privacy

PRIVACY

candy neubert

Shoestring Press

Printed by imprintdigital
Upton Pyne, Exeter
www.digital.imprint.co.uk

Typesetting by The Book Typesetters
us@thebooktypesetters.com
07422 598 168
www.thebooktypesetters.com

Published by Shoestring Press
19 Devonshire Avenue, Beeston, Nottingham, NG9 1BS
(0115) 925 1827
www.shoestringpress.co.uk

First published 2021
© Copyright: Candy Neubert
© Cover design and photograph: James Kipling

The moral right of the author has been asserted.

ISBN 978-1-912524-83-9

Contents

privacy

I have come home.
This room is my room
and the wind, restless outside,
driving the sea hard against the shore,
is mine,
and the salt smell
driving into my nose, mine,
and the bus which so slowly passed
hedges and field, the tractor turning left,
is mine, and when the driver says
do you want to get out here
I do
and the man in reception
is handing me the key.

navigating

Let's board a boat, shall we,
and then forget the harbour.

We'll look back at nothing, and then wonder
is it the wind or a current, taking us so fast?

Let's wait for dark, and have no oars,
or rudder even, and a bare mast.

tennis

I have preferred
the practice wall
and not the netted court

a decent racquet
and a ball
the steady thump
of steady thought
and no one else at all

inlet

There's only one coastline to trace again;
that is what happens when you dream islands.
Mostly it's high tide, the water milk green
right over the road, deep on the slipways,
sunlight moving slow across the sea wall
between bits of weed. Turning the corner
the air is sharp, the horizon purple.
This isn't happiness you remember,
but longing; how the cold of that water
takes the skin, how love is an obsession,
they say. They can use any word they like.
See those small white cottages – one of them
is yours; float from one inlet to the next
over and over, trying all the doors.

distant ship

No man may be an island; nonetheless
I am. A blur on the far horizon
looks promising to anyone at sea
striking out trustfully from their own rock.
They wash up here, disappointed to find
the place deserted, nothing much to eat,
no shelter worth speaking of, just the odd
tree. Others form whole archipelagos
wedged together by the shifting mantles
of love, but there's a spot of land out here
barely discernible in the sea mist.
Radar on shipping pick up a small blip;
their captains through binoculars may see
a figure on the beach, shaking her fist.

departure lounge

My suitcase blasted on the sand;
that folded shirt, those summer shoes,
down where the desert meets the sea,

mile after mile,
the rippled lines of wind
shifting the dunes.

Clouds go by over the Namib.
Little shadows hurry to be gone
across the moon.

Anyone there? Hello? No one.
No human loneliness
touched here.

I see it clear,
about to turn myself to bone,
rivet by rivet from the sky.

shoal

It was years ago I swam in the west
when the sun went down and waves
lifted a shoal of fish, the light behind them
catching each one gold.

So long ago you can't remember
if you swam with me or it was someone else
or I was just there by myself
and told you later. I was definitely

there and waves came up
over and over smooth and high
and broke on me and came again
with fish in, and behind them, light.

how to get a life

let me tell you there is nothing better
almost nothing better than getting into bed
in the middle of the afternoon
when the sun shines down outside
and you are perfectly well
shedding your clothes
one arm under the pillow
having no sense of ambition
beyond this experiment with quiet
having learned something from the cat
herself curled up under a garden bush

swim

This is a long marriage;
here's my husband,

I wade into him.
I stand respectful, worshipping,

my skin announces him,
flushes.

I was a child bride,
learned this rippling,

how whip-up waves run shade
along the sand,

make little shifts
like breathing in,

take hold of me
and lift and lift,

are good to me,
and weaken me.

I come up strong;
this is a long marriage.

plank

Turning the corner where the house La Roche
lies down long and white, lower than the road
by the Marais, where the sea defences
are a ridge of stone dotted with marram,
I found a plank. I think it was that place –
it may have been the Perelle headland
along the coast, not exactly a beach,
more a wind-battered, unfrequented spot,
the plank washed up bleach white, a careful heap
of pebbles either end. Old island lore.
As with husbands, as with wives, important
in a little place to be mindful of
and understand the signs. The pebbles mean
Hands off. I saw it first. This one is mine.

long back yard

This must be how we die, a Sunday train,
late afternoon, November, Basingstoke.
This must be how the heart falls out of reach
where it won't be warmed, too many faces
at the window getting on, getting off,
while we are all always between stations
staring out at hedges in case a fox
saves us. Here's a row of blue trampolines
in the long back yards, someone's bath cleaner
on an inside sill; here against this glass
in front of each of us the self's own shape
delivers a skull. Then out through the town;
an odd tree illuminates the dark,
the smell of leaf on stone, a reprimand.

rope

I am released from the family table
now. From those white plates

and second helpings and
the joined bending of heads.

Whiskers touch the pool,
watchful, listening to the bush.

Walking away from the kill
over the short, dry grass.

resurrection

so my mother you who have finally
lived long enough on this earth to discover
nothing matters in this whole world whatsoever

let us now walk out together
in the wonder and amazement of the garden

sink your head down there my mother
that is deep and cold and dandelion
and every stem of it bends
powerless and glad beneath its sun
and is a sheet of light and is the lawn

lean into it – fall in it like a girl
or like a bird
        unfold the ladder of your body
here my mother look the aching soil
delivers little shoots
their white roots bursting in a bed
whole fists of them threading
their way of silence under stone

silence my mother we have come upon
the pond
the tiptoes of our shoes
stilled by this flat surprise where
bugs lie under mud and without air
they have been wintering

and waterweed next month next week
rises my mother rises and the dandelion
and all the little shoots
        and all the green grass
rises

sea view

It was the agony of February did it
standing at the window looking out
the yellow wind eating the beach
the inside of his house
with sand blown in
while he made
fire
blast in the woodburner.

comb

I change the colour of my coat
slow as an arctic fox
ready to blend
into the snow

I am a ptarmigan
edging a plump and golden summer
mottling my feathers
for the cool white times ahead

the ocean waits for broaching
mile upon sea mile of chopped surface
more awesome with each year
bound to the shore

back lanes

he says you're lucky you have a good brain
as he walks me home along the back lanes
between the hedges where I long to go
the circular beginnings of mouse holes
the closed entrances where sparrows fly in
safe to another world I imagine
as I lie flat and look up through the leaves
considering this is what the word pleached
looks like just as peering into the grass
downwards gives a secret view of small paths
dipping here and there but always denied
to those such as myself on the outside
left with the task of using gracefully
this lucky brain whatever that may be

here are pebbles

She tries to get nearer; she moves along
the rows in the fine dust of the greenhouses,
slowly watering the base of each plant.
Back in the kitchen an hour before,
picnic things into a basket, a fold
of towels, the hour which made this hour
following to the path's end and the rail
where she leans, waiting. At the same moment
here are pebbles, cool from the falling tide,
slow back somersaults in the green water
– all of it here, gradually unpacking,
sandwiches in their foil, a paper bag
of tomatoes. Sand. Light. None of it gone,
none of it lost, none of it even past.

the harbour

I said time
between island and island
was time timeless
but it seems you did not see.
Important I explain
you understand
about the drops of land
we come across.

At the beginning is the harbour
with the many steps;
a telephone at night,
the trunks of trees and crates
along the quay. The tide laps up
and falls for miles, downward,
when it falls. Lean out between the houses,
see how far, and what strange green from
centuries before.

That is the harbour
with the soundless ships. Below
the concrete and the wood are always wet,
the dripping smell of world
and weed left hanging by the fuse
of pillars with the sea.

So many people leave this way.
Some in a hurry, though the lives of men
create no echoes here. Sometimes
a Chinese water boat will bear
a row of silent heads;
sometimes I sit across the walls
with legs on either side

and high winds pick me off.
I have been watching at the harbour
since a child, and since before that time.
He often comes this way.

There is a boat that leaves each day
though years may come between
the rising of one gangplank and the next,
the metal link through link around a wheel.

I nearly took the boat the day
it sank chaotic in the harbour mouth.
I ran to see it pull away
with sucking motion from the dock
and heave before the open sea,
before the eyes
of all the sudden crowd along the rail.

Of many hands at work to pull
the bodies from the water, I was one.
Not grieving for the dead, nor glad for life,
we worked in rhythm and the rain;
I heard them say too bad for you,
they said that you were there,
they brought you streaming up from stone
and laid you on the pier.

The home town rises up,
exultant in the moment crossed
from dream to death.
The wet cold sand, salt smell, the level sea,
the path of sun in triangles
that yield and pull, mid-ocean.

This is the harbour of the heaving line
slap slapping in the smell of oil,
the lifting ships, the men leap
one to one, a little drunk;
the tiny fish in clouds under the dock.

Another port to pass.
There goes the telephone,
here comes the music, up the mast and cables
snapping in the wind.

This is the harbour,
there the steps,
this is the way,
there is the helping hand.

Important you should know
just how it was to leave
and turn inland,
as those preparing for the sea
survive the land.

Important you should know
just how it is to leave the harbour,
being sure there is a cause,
that something matters beyond any doubt.

afternoon

On the way from one rock pool to another,
imagine someone calls.
Right in the middle of a bright afternoon,
with the sky grey in a far corner
                        and the sea beckoning,
your own name called.

You can't disobey but you can be difficult.
You can drag all the way over the stones
                        and across the sand,
up the steps, into the car park,
all through the unlocking of the door
                        and the back seat.
Time to leave.

Down the corridor we go. There's a hand
                        under your arm
and you're heading somewhere.
Come along, says the voice, but you drag
                        all the way.
Who cares about the day finishing; who knows
about a bright afternoon left in the middle
and the sea beckoning, and your own name?

married

Summon the out of season guest houses
lined up along an English promenade,
almost in a beautiful place, but not.
Call the apprehensive terraces laid
close to the railway station, promising
a new life that will open somewhere else
recently arrived here, come to a stop,
dropping a suitcase in a narrow hall,
the landlady and her husband slowly
ascending from the basement out of breath,
fumbling for a key. Seemed a good idea,
the rumbling train, the glitter of the sea;
why do we sit here in this dining room
reading the *Vacancies* sign inside out?

Atlantic

It can do your head in, looking at maps.
It becomes space and time, the chair covers
slightly furrowed, pouring like waterfalls
down its fat sides. I nestle between them,
willing myself into the Atlantic,
a breathtaking place, not merely no people
but nowhere for me to put my feet down,
not even a little barnacled rock,
only the sweep of continental shelf
sliding from pale blue to dark to purple.
Just turn on your back when you get tired
says my father; let the sea hold you.
I do, spreading my arms and looking up
through sky, or time, into my own face.

hostage

Your hair has grown. Grown like a meadow
of dry grass. It needs a trim; they will not
let you. Use a pin. For mine, we ask.
Sí, they say, bringing scissors.
Eduardo watches from the corner chair.
You lift, snip, tidy my neck and laugh,
remembering the last haircut you had
in Madrid. All the time Eduardo has
his carbine on his lap like a grey cat;
seems not to know it's there. Smiles,
smokes a cigarette, while you cut my hair.

I mark time carefully. The roof that was
alive with birds is quiet; they have flown.
I pray they will not move us yet, I pray
to hear the birds come back,
to feel the year. We are grown thin –
I look down on a lean flank, but
we like the food now, the strange
grains, Maria's soups; our mouths have
come alive. Your mouth near mine is like
a feeding fish. They leave us, give us
privacy. Our seed falls into rock.

We hear them talk, argue, drop things.
Trucks deliver, roosters crow.
Distance. Quiet. For us, such quiet.
In the beams gleam feathers, nails.
The birds up in the roof have flown,
have flown. The photographs and tapes

will keep the world away.
I need to say: forget us now;
we have a whole silence under these
rafters, in this bed, these shelves –
we swallow it all up and we
survive, even without trees.

I did not say it. We looked into
the lens and smiled and waved
and you were silent too, for me.

last wishes

It helps to know that other things have died.
A torn wing on the path, the small black lives
lost in a pool of rain, all passed
through that most curious divide.

It's hard to know that other things live on.
Birds singing now; that tree
cored in a deep green life. And you,
sure you will hear from me.

single daughter

There are sentences of death here,
and tall memories, and god.

Fruit trees ready to fall,
under-lit by headlights.

Against the wall, a bicycle.
My mother wants to ride away

but she is eighty-four,
held by the enemy.

I am the only one to hear.
The children sleep so deeply

and the old people are deaf.
Knock knock on the door.

Footsteps in the gravel as I
wait, holding my breath.

passing Jack's house

After a whole day of it I go out,
passing his shut gate and empty windows
– never a drawn curtain, never a light,
not so much as a pale blue glimmering;
nothing to suggest an old man, living.
Only his potatoes in their grey rows,
onions with a shadow strip of moonlight.
No dog, no cat, no wife now, a daughter
somewhere; I think he said Newton Abbot.
Maybe a radio on, maybe not.
I learn to turn mine off before the news
and let evening come, getting used to this,
how the unremarkable trees soften
out there, doing nothing, seeing no one.

sleeping with the Field Marshal

He makes cold company, but he and I
are all alone in a bare room. Outside,
someone in a far garden mows a lawn
and he turns his gaze towards the window
wistfully, above a high stiff collar.
Maybe some boyhood memory stirs
under the weight of those medals, the Cross
of something, the Order of something else.
I couldn't move him if I wanted to,
a woman stretched out, a warm afternoon,
plenty of those no doubt; no, it's the scent
wafting in, the blind rattling softly.
The mower stops, starts. I swear I see him
sigh under the epaulettes; a small frown.

this is a message

As I make my way
to the greenhouses
a lone gull kills me in its pure white throat.

Quiet in the tomatoes.
Quiet among the beans.
Soft dark patches where the rain leaks in.

Can I come home?
Has it been too long?
Tall weeds growing through the coils of hose.

pharmacy

I trust her look
the shadows round her eyes
her level stare
explaining paracetamol
these ones are strong
take them at night
she looks straight at me
she is not very tall either

inside
deeper than skin
confidence blooms
more fragile
and more certain
than the hug of a friend

burial

I walk through the Old Burying Ground
carrying the picnic
dreaming I am laid under the gum trees
in the still of night.

Tip me in shallow
where the graves collapse
next to all those
lost at sea.

How much would a sea burial cost
I wonder
as I arrive at the beach late
and you look at me, anxious.

materia medica

Changeable mood, silently brooding,
this is you. *Globus hystericus. Sleep,*

very light. Do you have dreams?
insomnia from grief and dreams continuing

and troubling. What grief and dreams?

You have a headache? Left or right?
A thirst? Worse in the morning, night?

For you, the St Ignatius Bean
as indicated. Why refuse? I have it

here. I'm at the bottom of the stairs

where I have opened every box
and turned the labels round for me,

for Apis Mel., the Honey Bee:
Whole brain is tired. Sensation as if

torn inside, of swallowing a howling fox.

low water

This is the place. Under the flat wet land
the ghost of a sting ray. Touch it, he says,
looking with interest at the limp tail,
the eyes askew. It's all flab and shudder,
not for the touching, not with her small hands
and their tiny gold hairs, but she can run
between the rocks which stand glistening brown,
drowned, six hours before, under three fathoms.
She tries it out, she walks in melting glass
over the sea bed, raising puffs of sand,
letting her hair float free in the current
while the sun warms the top of her head.
Don't struggle, he shouts, but she doesn't hear.
The sting ray ripples past, silent, lovely.

channel

sat on the sea wall as if all the world
was everywhere a sea wall and the sand
always spread out at my feet into light
and rock and rockpools and the bright channels
unroll their way down to a falling tide
as if always the heat of this long day
lay in the stone under my thighs as if
my skin would carry the crisp burn of salt
my shin and ankle bone be rough with it
my body ready to run into it
tomorrow or later or again now
as if thirst would anywhere only be
broken by this pushing out of my depth
out of my self out into open sea

ferry

We wait for the gangplank; it will be
down there, the steps under the pier
with their wetness and echo.
I find my place amidships
then as far forward as I can,
making the crowd disappear, an old trick
from way back. We wait for the tide
or a signal, balanced perfectly.

Always this engine
purring up my spine, always
these little fish. I sit
on a slatted locker gummed with salt,
bare feet on the rail, ready for spray,
ready for the rise and wallowing
which make some sick and me the opposite;
that other thing.

granite

She stands at the sea wall, its stone
holding the sun, the early morning cold,
and yesterday's sun, deepest of all.
The wind is at her legs; she pulls the towel,
a salt smell in its fibre, from the stone,
and from the sand.
The sea spreads out, cupped far away
in the open palm of the land.

Down there, alone, the high tide barely turned
and swilling at the wall, the boy stands,
hugging his surfboard.

He looks back over his shoulder,
making sure she watches him in this wide sea
to pin him to the surface, to exist. And she
is him, not only leaning on the wall
but down there too, cold water at her waist.
And time between
the standing at the wall and in the sea
becomes one thing which curves,
its two ends meeting, easily.

elephant

I want to kiss the elephant,
the young bull elephant behind the ashram,
pulling at his stakes.

A devotee's gift, struggling with himself.

Each day the boys will take him through the gate
and a little way into the forest.
On holy days they paint his head and drape his back
with the long bright cloth,
the tassels swung between his legs.

Now it is a warm, still, Indian night.

Staked to the ground by his four feet,
the teenage elephant thinks himself alone,
but I am here
standing in the mosquito dark.
I want to kiss him on the mouth, and take it from there.

80 sq yds per gallon

Nothing brings him to the door
quite as surely
as Silexine Watertight,
the complete waterproofer.
One Imperial Quart.

Opened this morning
to seal a stump,
it scents my hands
beyond washing.

No warning on the tin,
no list of toxins,
only a metal lid
scummed with rust.
Eleven and thruppence.

My father walks into his garage
and puts it away
on the back of the bench,
next to the spare.

chamber

The gun I keep in the underwear drawer
has a short grip; my little finger slips
right off the end of it. There are the four
chambers – it is like a heart, and it sits
well. It is for the white whale in my bed,
for taking him at night along the track
where rocks and pools long for him. Rounded lead
for the white marble mountain of his back.
The gun I keep in the underwear drawer
says Long John Silver; it might not be real
but it has a grey, unhappy colour
on the barrel and a sulphurous smell.
This helps him overcome the bashfulness
he feels about his size, and to undress.

ways to leave

Couldn't imagine, ducking from the porch,
hurrying through the yard with the lantern,
finding the nail to hang it just inside
the barn door, all hay, muck, and animal,
saying some quiet words, running a hand
down her ready flank, sorting out the tack,
saddling up, familiar rub of leather
through fingers, slipping the halter, snuffing
the lamp, always with the same quiet words,
all right there good girl fine girl, never mind
a bit of rain tonight, we have to leave,
now off we go, and hooves sound on the lane,
this very lane where no one could conceive
these keys, ignition, headlights, radio.

kindling

The big red dog
in the wood
is a fox.

Explains
the oval prints
in the snow-fresh lanes.

I think she is
a she
like me.

Maybe
she watches me
snap sticks.

I keep away
from new dug
earths.

I'm quick
in case
this place
is hers.

approaching America

our pilot on the Delaware
offers to show you
his laptop

these are the buoys, he says;
I know exactly where I am
to within a metre

this is the same way we track
our missiles
and bombs

you stare
for a moment
and say oh

then remembering your manners
add
thank you for showing me

Friday

I have people to see
is what I said.

I did not say
they are all in my head.

I am committed;
did not say to whom,

did not say to my own self
in my room.

I have places to be
where I must go.

You want to make arrangements?
Sorry, no.

canaries

In the Plaza de Asturias at noon a woman
runs up the steps to be photographed, smiling,
and a thin girl sits on the next bench
with a man who lays his head in her lap,
one arm around her back at the same time.
A little later she protests: *señor!* and takes off
between the trees, looking back once,
but the man lies on the seat, finished with her.
Another nearby reads Kahlil Gibran; the waiter
with the long black trouser legs walks round and round,
two men with cigarettes stroll by with prams
and there are girls, and birds, which are canaries.
On the flagstones at my feet, spit.

The girl comes back, walking slowly, kicking dust,
dipping her fingers in the fountain
and flicking them over the man, but she's already
fixed and written and the spit dry,
the man not only finished with her by now –
he's fast asleep with his hat over his face,
and even though the canaries are still singing
she can sit as long as she likes over there,
gazing at the man who has something she wants,
like the other end of a bad quarrel perhaps,
or money; however long she sits it's clearly
too late, spreading her hands in annoyance
as if the world is watching, which I am.

shed

Whatever I have done in the kitchen,
however wrong I am in the bathroom,
what false steps follow me down the High Street
finding there is no safe passage after
the possibility of being seen
by someone who has figured who I am,
unexpectedly caught in the muffle
of the check-out where I hear my name called
quite clearly far above the ringing,
coming home to find it an uncertain
place after all – whatever I have done,
a miracle has forgiven me here
as I pull open the door of the shed,
the crows on the rise into the branches.

fox

I hadn't thought of stopping but the sun
draws me to the warmer side of the hill
ten yards from where I know she has her place,
the fresh earth scrabbled from a big beech root
pale against the dark of a winter wood.
I sit a long time before I reach out
and touch a tree and then a whole ocean
wants to push out my eyes and I still sit,
wondering at this new thing, how the hunter
makes my hands lift up to cover my face
and how the spear finds me in the cold fields,
pinning me here until I'm sure that she
is curled beneath me somewhere small and round,
her hard red sleep a radiance in the ground.

ashes

I made you promise
to put my dead body in a boat
and set it alight

you were good with petrol and wood
you could lift any old dinghy
your hands were made for the job

I ran round to your house
with my eyes all mad
and made you promise

I said promise you won't let me
get stuck on this island not even my ashes
I won't be able to breathe

you looked up from your varnishing
and sighed and said yeah yeah

epiphragm

surprises me
how tight it holds the lane
this hot July

its circling trails
suggest confusion
in the deadly dry

and as I move it
to the cooler edge
I wonder why

not only will the snail
be saved by this
but so will I

review

(reading Daphne Rooke)

Thank you for the book. It reminded me
in the way she writes, dry as the Karoo,
of the long hot drive from Majiesfontein
the day Paul stopped to give a girl a lift
even though she wasn't expecting one.
She sat uneasily in the front seat
beside him, saying *thank you baas* until
he said don't call me baas I'm not your baas
and she said *yes baas*. That is how it was,
grit spattering the windscreen, fynbos, rock,
the shimmering air, the back of his neck,
all stuck in things as if we had been glued,
then flung to our invisible futures
which in my case would turn out to be you.

turtle

As if a turtle you have laid your eggs
in a bowl of sand. Unlike the turtle
you sit next to your own heap overlong
considering the wondrous thing you've done,
the babies wrestling in the gritty dark.
And all the while the land cools steadily,
a small white light somewhere over the sea,
over the sea out there and finally,
deeply and slowly you remember it.
You're setting off now. Here are your paddles,
this is the pale underneath of your shell
scraping the pebbles beneath the moon's glare.
Yourself, one thing alone now. Can you feel
the water's lift? You are already there.

playground

Hold on tight, they said, but you have moved on,
way beyond that. After a life on swings,
look - no hands; they are folded in your lap
quietly. Everything is quietly,
the air quietly sifting over your skin,
the bend of your knees imperceptible,
slight; the movement is all from the core,
from the torso. Forward, back, forward, back,
become almost bird-like, sifting the sky
on the stillness of wings, no more than thought
drifting there. A pigeon comes into sight,
flung from a tree with a burst of applause,
clap, clap, clap, and stop, before the swoop and drop.
Your next ambition, that exquisite pause.

dinner at the Grand Hotel

How many come before me? Although this
is a strange way to arrive, having told
no one. Perhaps it is all in my head.
Meanwhile I sit here in a stunned silence,
watching the waiters, watching how the sun
falls through the glass. Outside, the esplanade
fills me with such joy I can hardly breathe.
I may wait endlessly for the right word
to describe what this evening light achieves
on the white table cloth, where it lingers.
Seeing this light, transported by this air,
I am alive, I am alive, my dear,
receiving my hunger for solitude
as a gift, before I dip my finger.

praise

A single bed need not be hard.
The mid, mid hours of the night
(small cream lamps in a pale wood room)
are a filled cup, a new drink.

Unplug the phone; leave it lying
like a white tongue on the floor.
Lock the door. That's silence, brimming.
You know why God was thought up.

spine

Before I arrive, I begin to walk.
Early morning. The steps above Rosaire
damp earth held into place by iron pins,
webbed, side to side. September already,
white beads of water on the harbour's crane,
a milk churn cooling on the farmyard stone.
Where were we? Up over the island's spine,
smell of the pines on a hot dusty track,
travelling as she did, turning her back
curled up in bed, away all afternoon,
facing the wall, better to concentrate.
She swings on a gate opening to a path,
empty. Also the heat, also the dust.
Before I leave, I follow, as I must.

morning

Here are the great stone steps you know so well;
their wet surfaces gleam in the blue light
burning singly in a garage forecourt.
You've sat a lifetime, or however long,
knees drawn up to your chin, patient, waiting.
Who can say how morning comes, but it does,
lifting you up, not even out of breath,
over the top step just as the sky melts.
This is the old town, beginning to stir.
Come in here; the wooden doors stand open
to the street and he sits at a table
reading a newspaper. *Morning,* he says.
He says your name. *Want coffee?* And you do,
you can, and most incredibly, you're safe.

Acknowledgements

Acknowledgements are due to *Poetry Review*, *Times Literary Supplement*, *Rialto*, the *Spectator* and *New Contrast* (South Africa), where many of these poems have previously appeared.